Michael Graves
Hanselmann House
Snyderman House

Residential Masterpieces 14
Michael Graves
Hanselmann House
Snyderman House

Text by Julie Hanselmann Davies
Edited and photographed by Yukio Futagawa/GA photographers
Art direction: Gan Hosoya

Copyright © 2013 A.D.A. EDITA Tokyo Co., Ltd.
3-12-14 Sendagaya, Shibuya-ku, Tokyo 151-0051, Japan
All rights reserved. No part of this publication may be reproduced,
stored in a retrieval system, or transmitted,
in any form or by any means, electronic, mechanical,
photocopying, recording, or otherwise,
without permission in writing from the publisher.

Copyright of photographs
©2013 GA photographers

Printed and bound in Japan

ISBN 978-4-87140-639-0 C1352

Residential Masterpieces 14

Michael Graves

Hanselmann House

Fort Wayne, Indiana, U.S.A., 1967-71

Snyderman House

Fort Wayne, Indiana, U.S.A., 1969-77

Text by Julie Hanselmann Davies

Edited and Photographed by Yukio Futagawa

世界現代住宅全集14
マイケル・グレイヴス
ハンセルマン邸　1967-71
アメリカ合衆国，インディアナ州，フォートウェイン
スナイダーマン邸　1969-77
アメリカ合衆国，インディアナ州，フォートウェイン
文：ジュリー・ハンセルマン・デイヴィーズ
企画・編集・撮影：二川幸夫

GA

マイケル・グレイヴスの初期の住宅
―― ジュリー・ハンセルマン・デイヴィーズ

The Early Houses of Michael Graves
by Julie Hanselmann Davies

マイケル・グレイヴスは，いわゆるポストモダンの方法における明快な幾何学的形態やヴォリューム表現，さらにこれらに付随する色彩とフォルムについて，最も頻繁に参照される世界的建築家である。古典建築のリズムとヒエラルキーに影響を受けたグレイヴスの建築は，古代の真実性に対する現代的再解釈である。インディアナの2棟の住宅に見られるように，グレイヴスの初期の作品は，最終的には成熟したスタイルへと帰着する形態への探究がはっきりと描かれている。

画家としての教育を受けたグレイヴスはハーヴァード大学へと進み，ローマ賞を授与された後，プリンストン大学で教鞭をとる。初期の数年間，グレイヴスはル・コルビュジエやモダニズムの原則を継承して研究を行ってきた。主に1920年代に試みられたこのようなモダニズムのアプローチは，機械化された20世紀の時代精神に触発された「新建築」の理念に基づき，過去の装飾的かつ過度に歴史的な建築を否定したことで知られている。工業製品の窓枠で分割された純粋な白のファサードを外皮にまとい，構造壁から解放された「自由な平面」。新しい精神が求めたのは「住むための機械」としてのピュリスムの構成である。この文脈において，住宅は「庭園の中の機械」として再構築された。その一方で，非常に凡庸な，模倣を強要する行為に対し，1960年代から70年代にかけて，建築家や理論家によるヨーロッパ・モダニズムに対する再評価が行われた。その結果は，知性に富み，深い洞察力と共に多くの議論を巻き起こした影響力ある作品群，例えばコリン・ロウの『透明性 実と虚』や『マニエリスムと近代建築』，あるいはニューヨーク・ファイブ（グレイヴス，ピーター・アイゼンマン，チャールズ・グワスミー，ジョン・ヘイダック，リチャード・マイヤーによる）の住宅へと結実することになる。

「ハンセルマン邸」
グレイヴスによるコルビュジエの住宅に関する初めての探究は，本格的に仕事の依頼を受けるようになったインディアナ州フォートウェインの「ハンセルマン邸」においてである。この作品は（とりわけ地中海を中心とした）ル・コルビュジエの描くヨーロッパ建築をアメリカ的文脈に再解釈した秀作である。典型的な郊外住宅地の1エーカーの区画の一角，木々に囲まれた敷地の最も高い場所にグレイヴスは住宅を置いた。車道から住宅にアプローチすると東面のファサードが現れる。三層の「キューブ」は広葉樹の森の中にその姿を見せる。白いファサードは，広大な空間，長く延びる帯状の壁面，垂直のスリットへと，全て叙情的な形態とプロポーションに分解される。住宅は近隣から背高くそびえるように建つ。小スタジオ（アクソメ・ドローイング参照）は建築されることがなく，したがってグレイヴスが意図した住宅正面の屋外「キューブ」は実現されずに終わる。とはいえ，屋外階段のステップを上がりブリッジへと続く劇的なエントランスにより，訪問者は空中からその構成を観賞することとなった。このスタジオ・フォリーはゲートハウスのようなもので，グレイヴスは，アテネのアクロポリスの丘に建つアテナ・ニケ神殿を参照し引用している。メイン・ファサードは，訪問者の通過する第二のレイヤーである。そして現象学的には透明な第三のレイヤーは，背後の壁である。ここにグレ

Michael Graves is now a world-renown architect of lush referential works in the so-called Postmodern mode, where form and color are attendants to a clear architectural expression of geometric shapes and volumes. Inspired by the rhythms and hierarchies of classical architecture, Graves reinterprets the ancient verities for his own time. His early work, as best shown in two Indiana houses miles apart, maps a formal investigation that eventually led to his mature style.

Graves began his architectural career with a painter's training, studies at Harvard, a Rome Prize, and a Princeton professorship. In the early years, he followed the teaching and example of Le Corbusier and the modernist canon. This modernist approach, developed primarily in the 1920s, rejected the ornamented and historically overwrought architecture of the past in favor of a 'new architecture' inspired by the zeitgeist of the mechanized twentieth century. Pure white facades sliced with industrial casement windows enclosed floor plans released from the tyranny of walls, the *plan libre*. The new spirit favored purist compositions of 'machines for living' and villas were reinvented as 'machines in the garden'. Decades of mostly dreary imitation compelled architects and theorists of the 1960s and 70s to re-evaluate European modernism. The result was a profound intellectual outpouring yielding seminal works like Colin Rowe's *Transparency: Literal and Phenomenal* and *The Mathematics of the Ideal Villa* and the mostly residential work of the so-called 'New York Five' (Graves, Peter Eisenman, Charles Gwathmey, John Hejduk and Richard Meier).

HANSELMANN HOUSE
Graves' investigation of the Corbusian villa began in his first major commission, the Hanselmann House in Fort Wayne, Indiana. The work represents a remarkable translation of Le Corbusier's European (and essentially Mediterranean) vision to an American context. On a corner one-acre lot in a typical suburban housing sub-division, Graves places the house at the highest elevation of the wooded site. The house's east facade greets you as you approach from the driveway. What you see is a three-story cube, set within a hardwood forest, its white surfaces broken with windows of all lyrical shapes and size— broad expanses, ribbons, and vertical slits. The house towers above its neighbors. Because a small studio building was never built (see axonometric drawing), Graves' intention to create a 'cube' of open space enfronting the house is somewhat lost, although the dramatic entrance via outdoor flight of steps and bridge lifts the visitor to a mid-air appreciation of the structure. This studio folly was intended as a kind of gatehouse, Graves citing the Temple of Athena Nike on the Athenian Acropolis as a reference. The main facade is the second layer that a visitor passes through; the third layer of this phenomenological transparency is the back wall. This is the sur-

イヴスは，建物とその居住者の物語を20フィート（約6メートル）の壁画として設置した。

住宅は2階がエントランスにあたる。グレイヴスは主要居室を構成するこの階を，ヨーロッパの伝統様式に見る「ピアノ・ノビーレ」として計画し，一般的に想定される現代的なアメリカ住宅のかたちを逆転させた。6人家族のために設計されたこの住宅が，簡素な床面積と比べて一層大きく感じられるのは，グレイヴスの彫塑的な二層吹き抜けの空間と，建築全体に及ぶ垂直方向の開放性によってである。開放的な平面計画は，リビングとダイニングに流れるようなつながりを生み出す。また，断面計画においても吹き抜けが劇的な眺めをもたらし，同時に太陽光を全ての階へと行き渡らせる。主寝室を最上階に，子供の居室を1階に計画したのは確かに革新的試みであった。この住宅では各々が孤立することなく，プライバシーが確保されている。

グレイヴスの作品がコルビュジエの住宅と比べて非常に異なるのは，楽しげなマッスの操作による点においてである。住宅の南東の角を切り取ることで，表面の白い外皮からセットバックした三層のガラスのファサードが見える。この壁の操作によって，最も素晴らしい眺望と太陽光が，惜しみなく内部へと引き込まれてくる。また，主寝室からブリッジで続く最上階の屋外空間も，同じように切り取られている。このルーフ・テラスでは「(現象としての)窓枠」が屋外の東面のファサードに，他方では（文字通りの意味で）本物の窓が，リビングを見下ろすように計画された。矩形の「窓枠」は，主寝室の張出しのガラス窓を正確に反転させて切り抜かれたものである。これらの叙情的なタッチは，建築のフォルムや機能に対する新しい翻訳的アプローチと相矛盾するものである。多義性とユーモアに対するスタンスは，ロバート・ヴェンチューリの多様性と対立性を想起させる。

また，ル・コルビュジエと比べて見ると，グレイヴスの建築作品は色彩に彩られているのが解る。「ハンセルマン邸」ではグレイヴスは色彩を使い，設計思想の説明を明快に行った。本質的に，グレイヴスは色彩を用いて物語を組み立てる。エントランス側のファサードの青のスパンドレルは敷地に流れる小川を参照したものである。同じ青色は再び最上階に現れる。小川にも似た緩やかな曲線を描く棚板は小径を想起させる。上階の天窓の下端は明るい黄色に塗装され，光に暖かみを与えると共に，太陽の輝きを思わせてくれる。主階の化粧室はプライベートな時間を過ごせるように，冗談まじりに草むらがイメージされ，鮮やかな緑で塗装されている。主寝室のベッド背後のクローゼットは干草色に塗装された。しかしながら彼の天性である画家的な才能がいかんなく発揮されたのは壁画であり，ここに建築上の主題が要約された。周囲の景観が参照されている。庭園部分は花柄のテーブルクロスさながらである。木々は藤色の影を落とし，猫の頭のシルエットもある。この家の形態と角度は全て壁画に現れ，実存を越えたキュビストの絵画表現を強く想起させる。

face where Graves placed a 20-foot mural that tells the story of the building and its inhabitants.

By entering the house on the second level, where the principal rooms are, Graves creates a *piano nobile* in the European tradition and thereby flips on its head the expectation of a contemporary American home. The house, designed for a family of six, feels much larger than its modest floor area, due to Graves' sculpting of double-height space and a remarkable vertical openness throughout the building's dimensions. The open plan creates a fluid communication between living and dining spaces while the double-height section affords dramatic views and allows sunlight to penetrate all levels. It was certainly an innovation to place the master bedroom suite on the top floor and the children's rooms on the ground floor. Privacy, while not absolute, was afforded by the separation.

It is in the playful manipulation of the house's massing that Graves departs most from the example of the Corbusian villa. He carves away the southeast corner of the house, revealing a three-story glazed facade set back from the outer white surface. This wall affords the best views out and lets in plentiful filtered sunlight. He carves out an outdoor room on the top floor, reached from the master bedroom by a bridge. This roof terrace has an open 'window' framed on the east facade (phenomenological) and real windows looking down into the living room (literal). A shape of a framed rectangular 'window' is cut out and mirrored by a glazed bay window of identical shape in the master bedroom. These lyrical touches belie this new interpretative attitude towards architectural form and function, a stance that embraces ambiguity and indeed humor. Robert Venturi's complexity and contradiction comes to mind.

Another attribute that aligns Graves' work to Le Corbusier's is the use of architectural polychromy. In the Hanselmann House, Graves uses color to elucidate further his architectural ideas. In essence, he tells a story using color. The blue spandrel on the entry facade is a reference to the stream that flows through the site. The same blue is repeated on the top floor, as a gently curved shelf parallels the stream and recalls its path. The soffit of the upstairs skylight is painted a bright yellow, warming the light and recalling the sun. The powder room on the main floor is painted a vivid green, a tongue-in-cheek reference to a bush, behind which one could find a private moment. The closet behind the master bed is a painted haystack. But the finest example of his painterly instinct is the mural, where he summarizes the themes of the architectural work. The surrounding landscape is referenced. A garden plot doubles as a floral tablecloth; trees cast a mauve shadow, there's a silhouette of a cat's head. The shapes and angles of the house are all recalled in the mural, which like a Cubist painting evokes without being literal.

「スナイダーマン邸」
「ハンセルマン邸」から数年が経ち，8マイル（約12キロメートル）離れた場所に計画された「スナイダーマン邸」は，グレイヴスの形態言語の転換点となった。残念ながら，この住宅は人が住まなくなってから数年の後，2002年に火事により焼失してしまっている。そのため現在では，この住宅に関する知識は写真や文章から収集されたものに留まっている。誇張表現を抜きにしても，この構造はグレイヴスの初期の作品の理想の極致と言ってよい。これは白色のモダニズムから多彩色のポストモダンへの移行を顕著に示すものである。ファン・グリスの絵画が三次元的に強い印象を与えるように，この住宅は住まいという概念を超越し，まさしく建築彫刻へと見事に変化させた。これは住宅の計画として，かつてないまでに特筆すべき建築的理念の提起であった。

40エーカーの広葉樹の森林の中央に計画された5人家族のためのこの住宅は，グレイヴスの事務所にとって非常に野心的な計画であった。このプログラムでは，「ハンセルマン邸」の時よりも大きなリビングと，ゲストをもてなすための非常にゆったりとした宿泊設備が要求された。一連の居室はその後，ゲストルームとして改装され，地上から直接アプローチすることができるようになった。

より大きく複雑なプログラムにおいては，グレイヴスはより表現力のある大胆な解決方法を提示している。グレイヴスの作品はコルビュジエの「庭園の中の機械」の概念から始まり，茂ったランドスケープの中でそれとは独立して置かれたサヴォワ邸に見られるような，初期のホワイト・キューブへと進む。2本の軸線が交錯する「起点」が，内部を構成する動線の出発点である。形態的な階段は軸線の交差するところ，この住宅の中心部に打ち込まれたアンカーとして機能する。階段は空間同士の関係性を「紡ぐ」ように全ての居室から眺めることができ，白いグリッドの軸組と色彩溢れる空間の中で舞い踊る。

グレイヴスはさらに，太陽の軌道に沿うように居室の計画を行った。東側の朝食室は一日の始まりを迎え，中心のリビングは南からの太陽光を独占するように配置された。1階の主寝室は，西向きに計画されている。グレイヴスは住宅全体に太陽光が行き渡るように，ファサードの操作を行っている。

平面と曲面，人工と自然，プライベートとパブリック，内部と外部，白色と多彩色。この建築に彩りを与えているのは，これら正反対の概念的要素の組み合わせである。森の空き地の中に佇む，珍しく，そして驚くべき生き物のようなこの住宅にとって，目に映るその瞬間がその物語の始まりなのだ。東面のファサードへと近づくと，多彩色のフォルムが三層の軸組の内外にわたり，曲線を描くようにその周囲を走る。入口の扉が幅の広い石板のテラスにセットバックして設けられ，すぐ上の突き出た雲のようなフォルムがその目印となっている。それは楽しげな効果を与えている。住宅は正面性を捨て，三次元の形態操作の戯れがどこまでも続く。大きくフラットな床面は波打つ壁面と対照を成す。ガラスの取り付けられていない開口部の窓枠からは，遠くの空と自然を見渡すことができる。リズミカルな階段は構造体の脇をジグザグに上がる。暖炉の煙道の役割を果たす三層吹き抜けの円筒は，

SNYDERMAN HOUSE

Eight miles away and a few years later, Graves' commission for the Snyderman family finds Graves pushing his formal language to a brink. Unfortunately, the house was destroyed by fire in 2002, after several years of abandonment. And so its lessons can now only be gleaned from photographs and descriptions. It is no exaggeration to deem this structure the apotheosis of Graves' early work. It marks his transition from white modernism towards polychrome Postmodern. A Juan Gris painting punched into three dimensions, the house veers so delightfully toward outright architectural sculpture that it begins to lose all sense of being a house. It was one of the most remarkable architectural visions ever brought to a residential project.

Set in the middle of forty acres of hardwood forest, this house for a family of five represents a more ambitious project for the Graves office. The program called for more living space than the Hanselmann House required, and also needed generous accommodation for entertaining. A suite of rooms needed to be converted later into guest quarters, with a separate access point from the ground level.

With a larger and more complicated program, Graves responded with a solution both more expressive and more daring. He started with the Corbusian notion of a 'machine in a garden', but gone is the pristine white cube sitting independently in a lush landscape, as with the Villa Savoye. The *parti* is organized from the inside, beginning with two crossing axes. A formal stair placed at the intersection of the axes acts as a spatial anchor at the heart of the house. The stair is seen from all rooms that conceptually 'spin' around this nexus, a formal dance between a white gridded framework and colored room-shapes that participate in a referential choreography.

Additionally, Graves placed the rooms of the house to follow the daily movement of the sun. And so in the eastern section a breakfast room greets the day, the main living rooms take up the areas with southern exposure, and a ground level master bedroom suite faces the westering sun. Throughout the house, Graves uses facade elements to control the sunlight as it permeates the building.

Then, what animates the architecture is a conceptual framework of opposites: flat vs. curved, man-made vs. the natural, private vs. public, interior vs. exterior, white vs. color. Upon first glimpse of the house, which sits like a marvelous, strange creature within a wooded clearing, these narratives are already at work. One approaches the eastern facade, where polychrome forms curve in, out and around a three-story-high white framework. The entry door is set back on a wide slate terrace, its presence signaled by a cloud-like form jutting out above. The effect is exuberant. The house resists frontality in favor of a restless three-dimensional formal play. Large flat

納屋とサイロを想起させる。視線のさまよう先には常に，複雑さと光と影の魅惑的な戯れが存在する。様々な色彩の諧調は内外の境界を消失させる。自然から色彩を引き出してくることによって，グレイヴスはこのような多義性を一層強く表現しているのだ。

　内部空間も同じように，流れるような躍動感で溢れている。階段にはグリッド状の大きな天窓から光が差し込み，空間を一体的に統合する。16世紀，フランスのシャンボール城の階段室に影響を受けたこの優雅な構成は，かつて試みられた階段室の設計のうちでも，最も優れたもののひとつである。階段室には天蓋のようなディテールが施されている。この入れ子状のミニチュアのような空間は，浮遊する平面，すらりとしたアーチ，彫塑的なスティールの装飾によって，囲われた感覚を生み出している。階段を行き来する経験は，光や色彩，表面や軸組が常に揺れ動く感覚を与える。それはまるでキュビストの絵画の中に住むようなものだ。

　ドローイングを通してこの建築の複雑性を想像することは，いかなる優れた空間への想像力をもってしても不可能である。「スナイダーマン邸」について理解するうえで最良の方法は，この住宅の中を歩くことである。それでもなお，繊細で深遠な空間の変化を十分に知覚するには及ばないだろう。この住宅が失われたことは大きな悲しみである。

　工期の延長を重ね，「スナイダーマン邸」の建設が進むにつれて，グレイヴスは，より根源的な建築理解から導き出された建築へ向かっていった。そこでは，いかなる理論的な提案も身体スケールこそが立脚点となる。公共建築を手掛けるようになり，グレイヴスはローマで学んだ教訓を一層明確に実践に移すことができるようになった。グレイヴスは現在，コルビュジエの理論モデルではなく古典建築をそのインスピレーションとして用いているが，モダニズムのアプローチを放棄することは決してなかった。住宅からオフィス・タワーに至るまで，あらゆる建築の実践はそれまでの経験の解釈によるものである。つまり，独創性とは，知的洞察と探究から生み出される。これらの初期の住宅作品においてさえ，グレイヴスは機知に富み，創造力豊かな手によって，名作を生み出してきたのである。

和訳：原田勝之

---

planes contrast with undulating walls. Openings punched in these surfaces are unglazed windows framing views to the sky and landscape beyond. Staccato staircases zigzag up the side of the structure. A three-story cylinder, which houses a fireplace flue, evokes a barn silo. Everywhere the eye travels there is complexity, a mesmerizing play of light and shadow. The color palette further collapses the separation between inside and outside. By deriving his colors from nature, Graves further emphasizes this ambiguity.

　The interiors are likewise fluid and dynamic. The stair, lit from above by a broad gridded skylight, unifies the space as its central core. Inspired by staircases such as the one at Château de Chambord from the sixteenth century in France, this elegant confection is one of the finest staircases ever conceived. It is detailed like a baldacchino, a miniature building-within-a-building, with a sense of enclosure implied by flying planes, slender soffits and sculptural steel ornament. The experience of rising and descending offers an ever-shifting play of light, color, surface, and frame. It is like inhabiting a Cubist painting.

　The complexity of this building is almost impossible to imagine through a study of the architectural drawings, even when done with the finest spatial imagination. The best way to understand the Snyderman House is to move through it, and even then it defies comprehension as the shifts in experience are so subtle and profound. Its absence is greatly felt, and mourned.

　While the Snyderman House was being built, over a protracted period, Graves began a transition to an architecture derived more exclusively from an understanding of architecture at its most elemental, where the scale of the human body was the starting point of any theoretical proposition. Work on civic commissions allowed him to exercise more specifically the lessons he had learned in Rome. While he now turned to examples of ancient architecture for inspiration instead of Corbusian models, he never abandoned an essentially modern approach to his work. The exercise of building anything from a family home to an office tower is an interpretation of former lessons; originality comes from intellectual insight and query. Even in these early examples of residential architecture, Graves was exhibiting the nimble mind and artful hand to create a masterpiece.

Hanselmann House 1967-71

Overall view from south

Overall view from east

View from southeast. Staircase to entrance

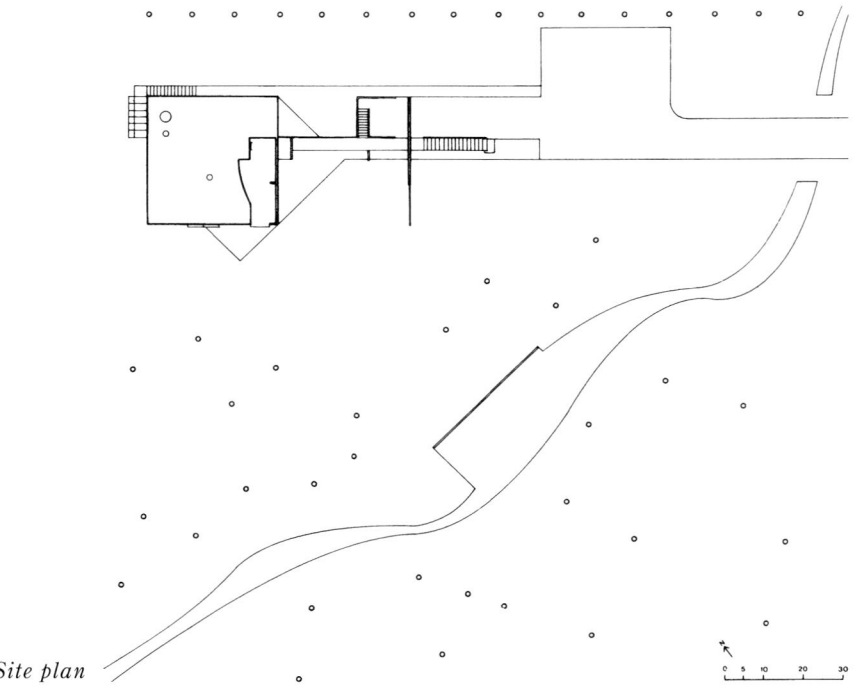

Site plan

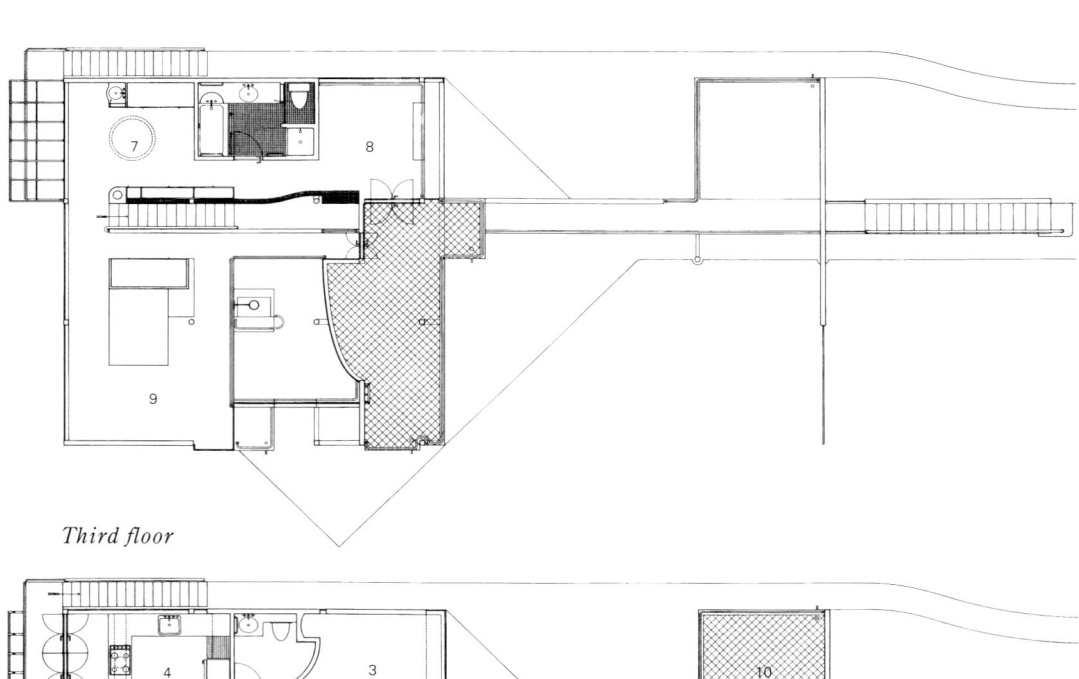

Third floor

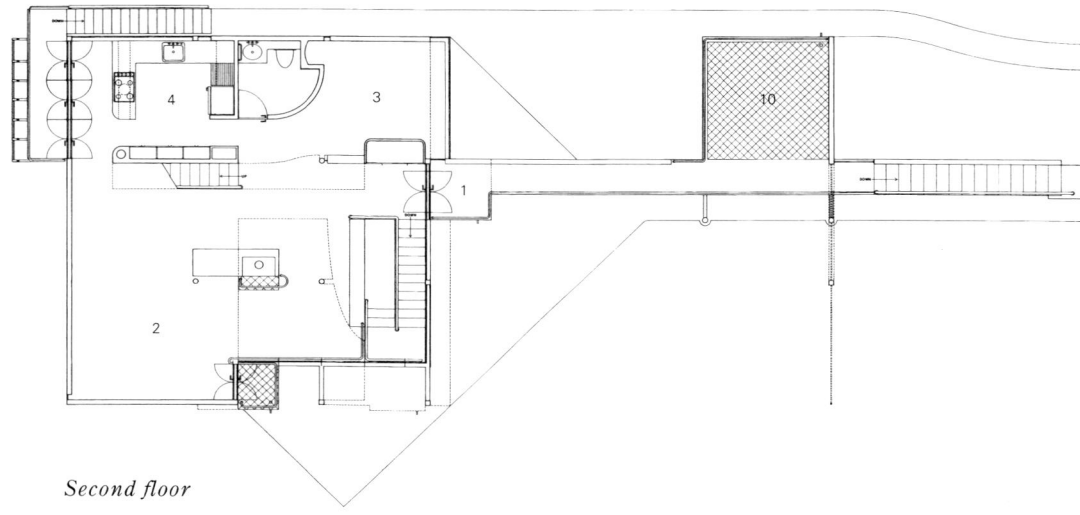

Second floor

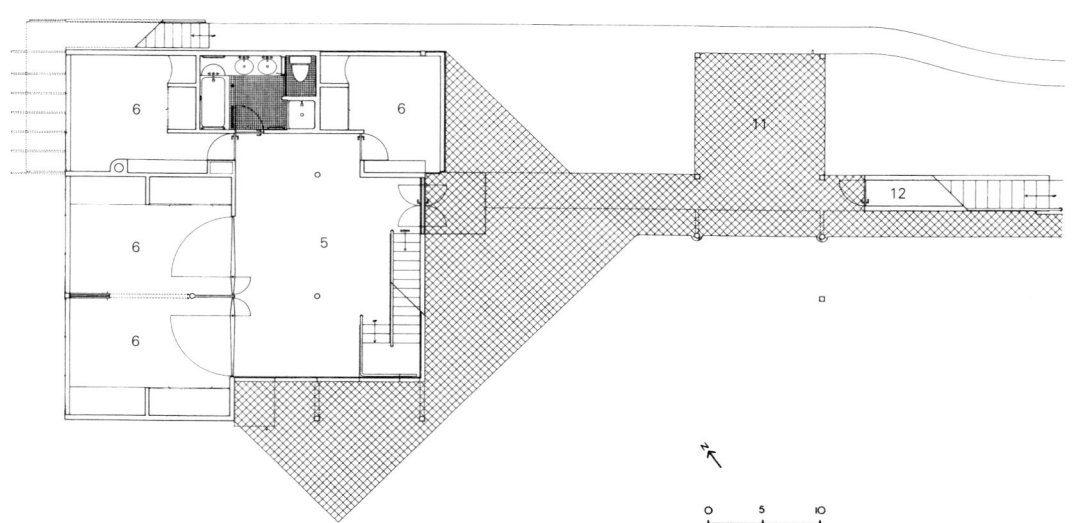

First floor

1 ENTRANCE
2 LIVING ROOM
3 DINING ROOM
4 KITCHEN
5 PLAYROOM
6 BEDROOM
7 DRESSING ROOM
8 STUDY
9 MASTER BEDROOM
10 FUTURE TERRACE
11 FUTURE STUDIO
12 STORAGE

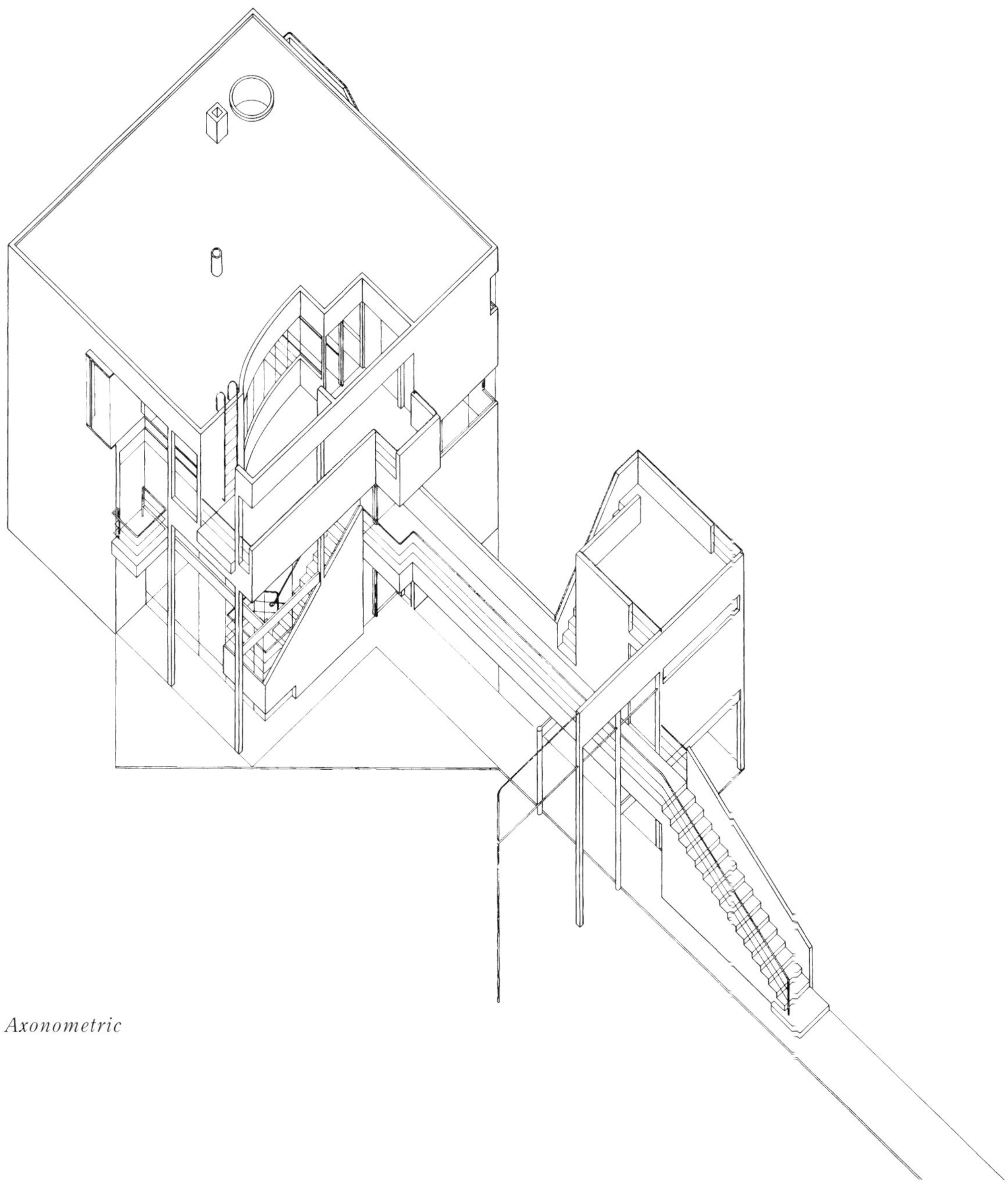

Axonometric

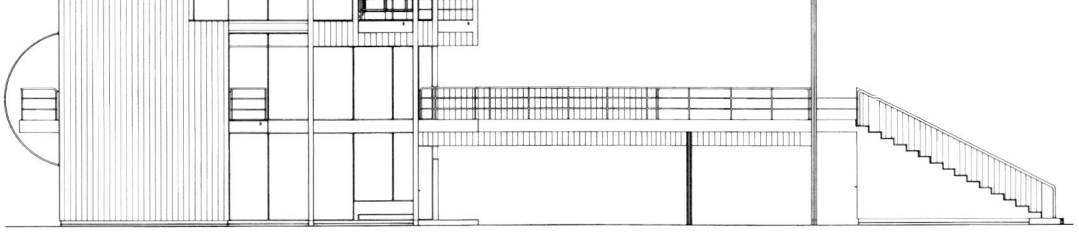

Southwest elevation

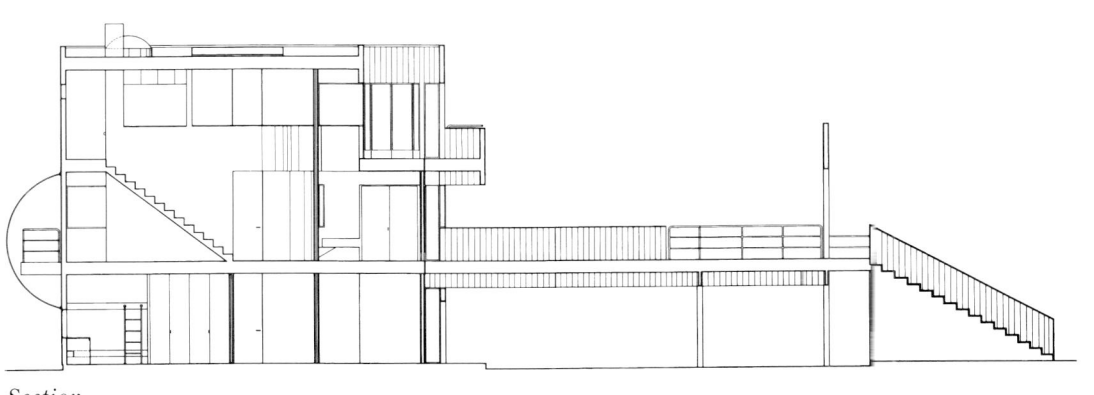

Section

South corner. View toward entrance bridge

South corner. View from entrance bridge

Southeast elevation

Southwest elevation

Northwest elevation

Living room. Mural by Michael Graves

Living room. View toward entrance

Dining room on right, bathroom on center

Living room. Looking southeast

Living room. Looking southwest

Downward view of living room. Staircase to first floor

View from dining room. Entrance on left

Kitchen

Staircase to third floor. Living room on left, kitchen on right

Master bedroom on third floor. Looking southeast

Master bedroom (left) and dressing room (right)

Third floor. View toward master bedroom from study

Third floor. View from staircase toward southeast

First floor. Staircase to entrance

Playroom on first floor

View from bedroom toward playroom

View toward bedrooms from playroom

Snyderman House 1969-77

Overall view from south

View from southwest

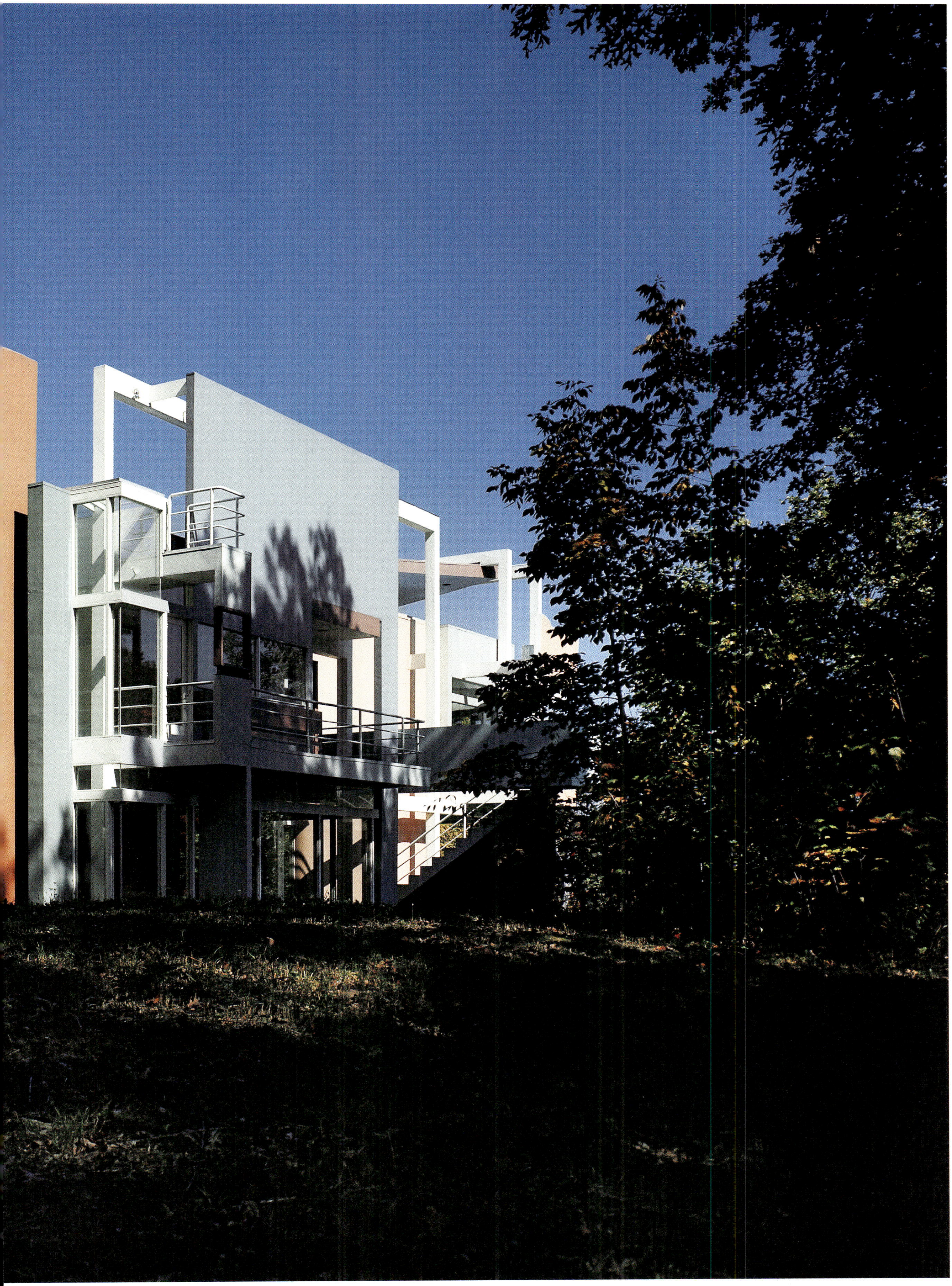

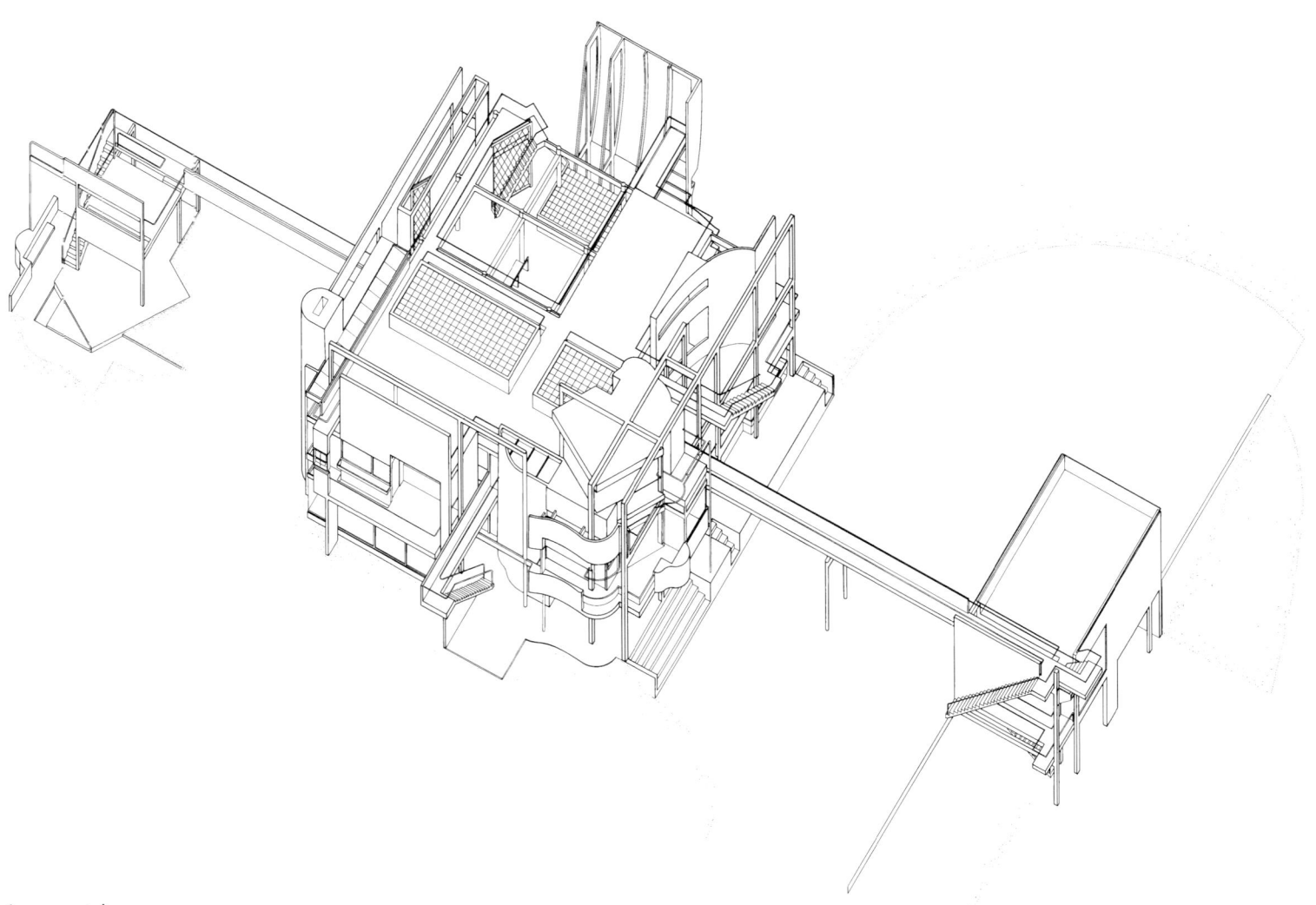

Axonometric

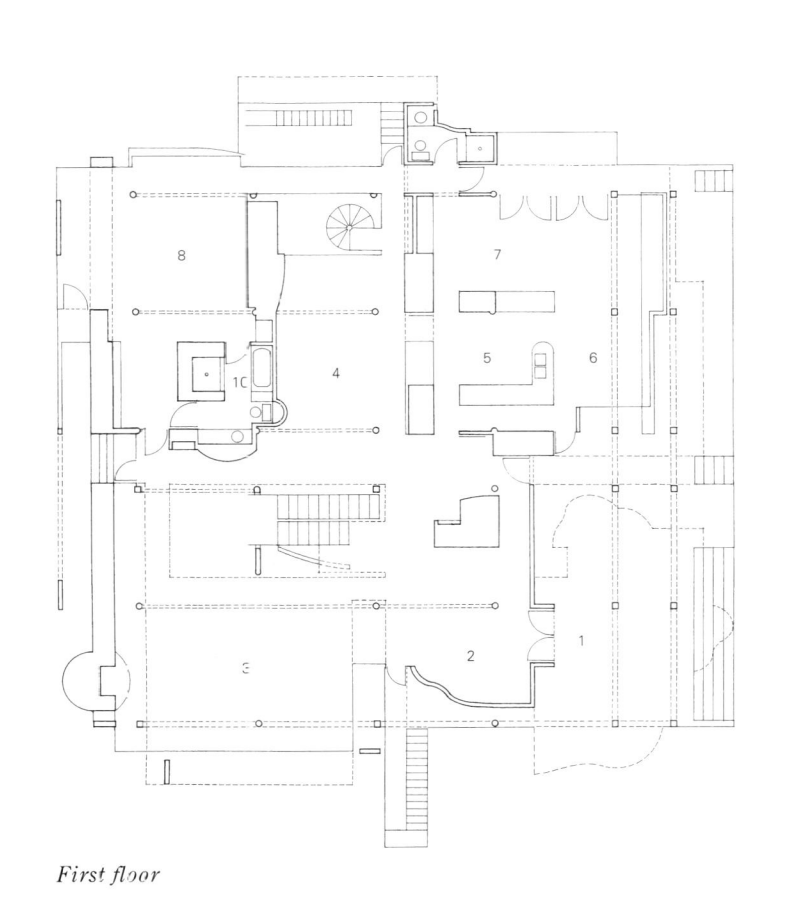

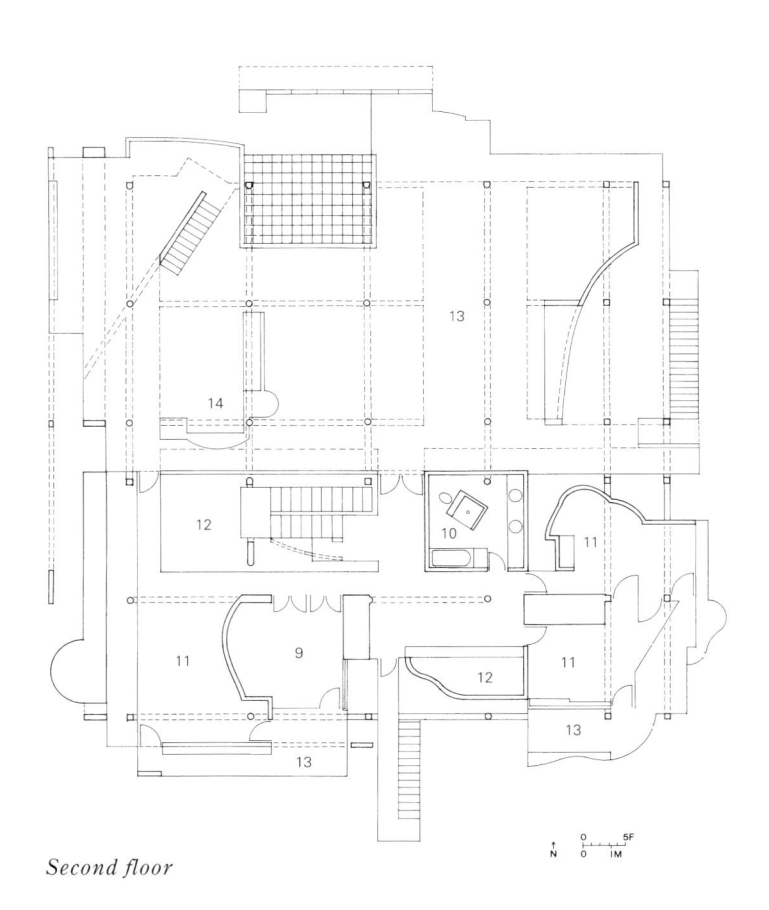

First floor

Second floor

Site plan

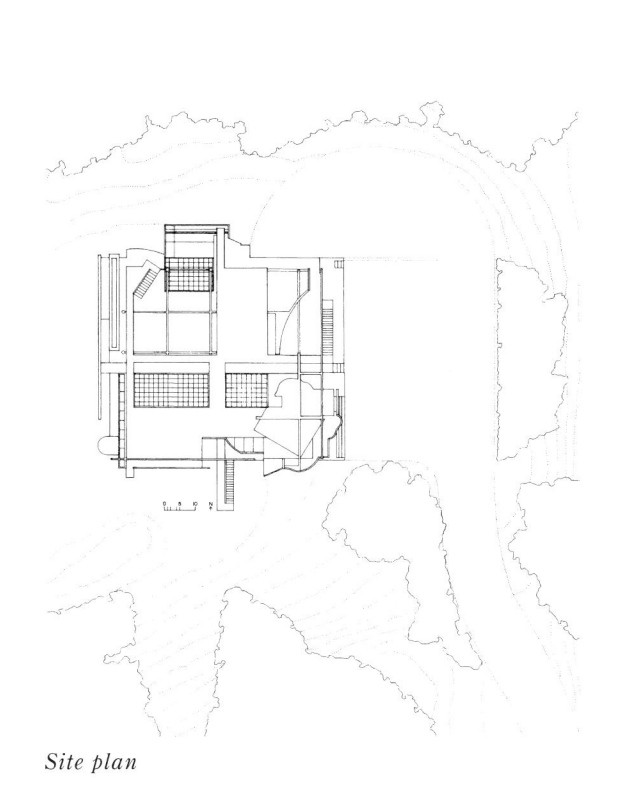

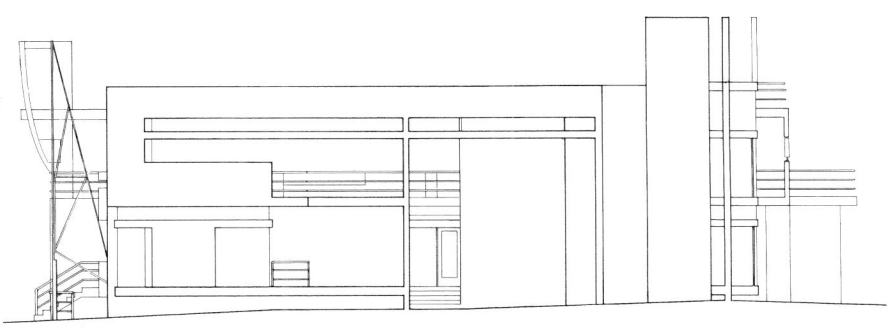

West elevation

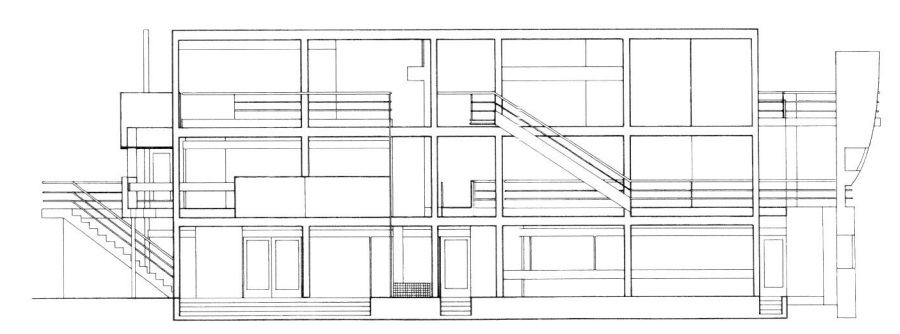

East elevation

1 ENTRANCE TERRACE
2 FOYER
3 LIVING ROOM
4 DINING ROOM
5 KITCHEN
6 BREAKFAST ROOM
7 FAMILY ROOM
8 MASTER BEDROOM
9 BEDROOM
10 BATHROOM
11 STUDY
12 VOID
13 ROOF TERRACE
14 TERRACE SEATING

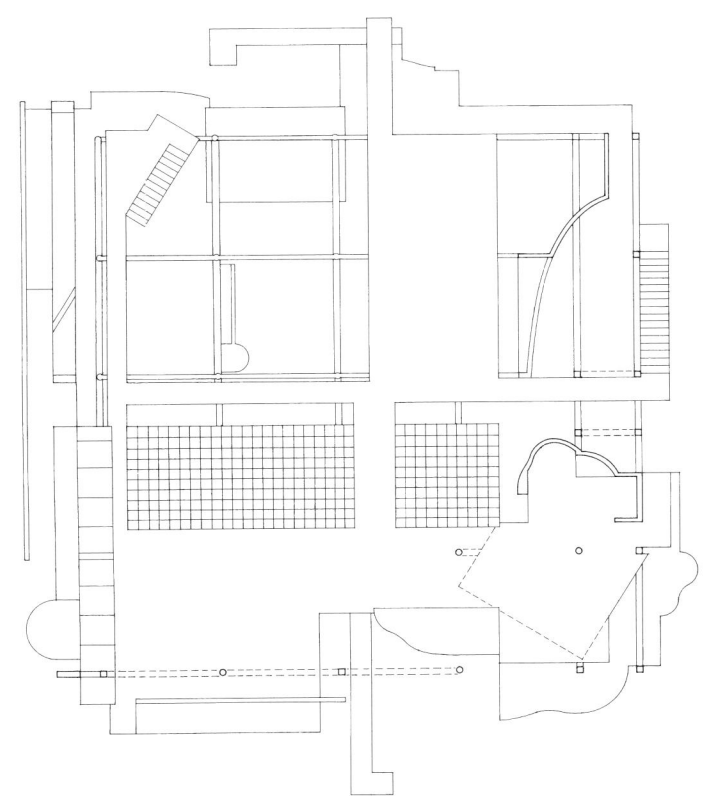

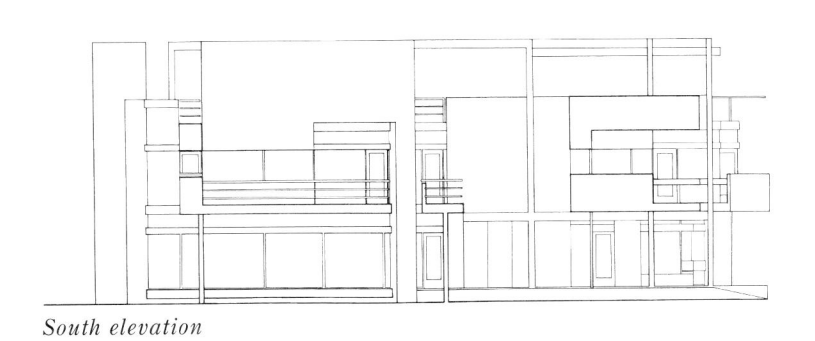

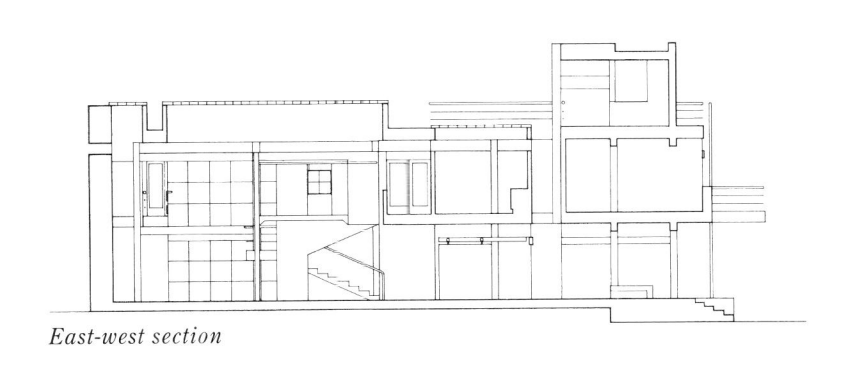

North elevation

South elevation

Third floor

East-west section

Partial south elevation

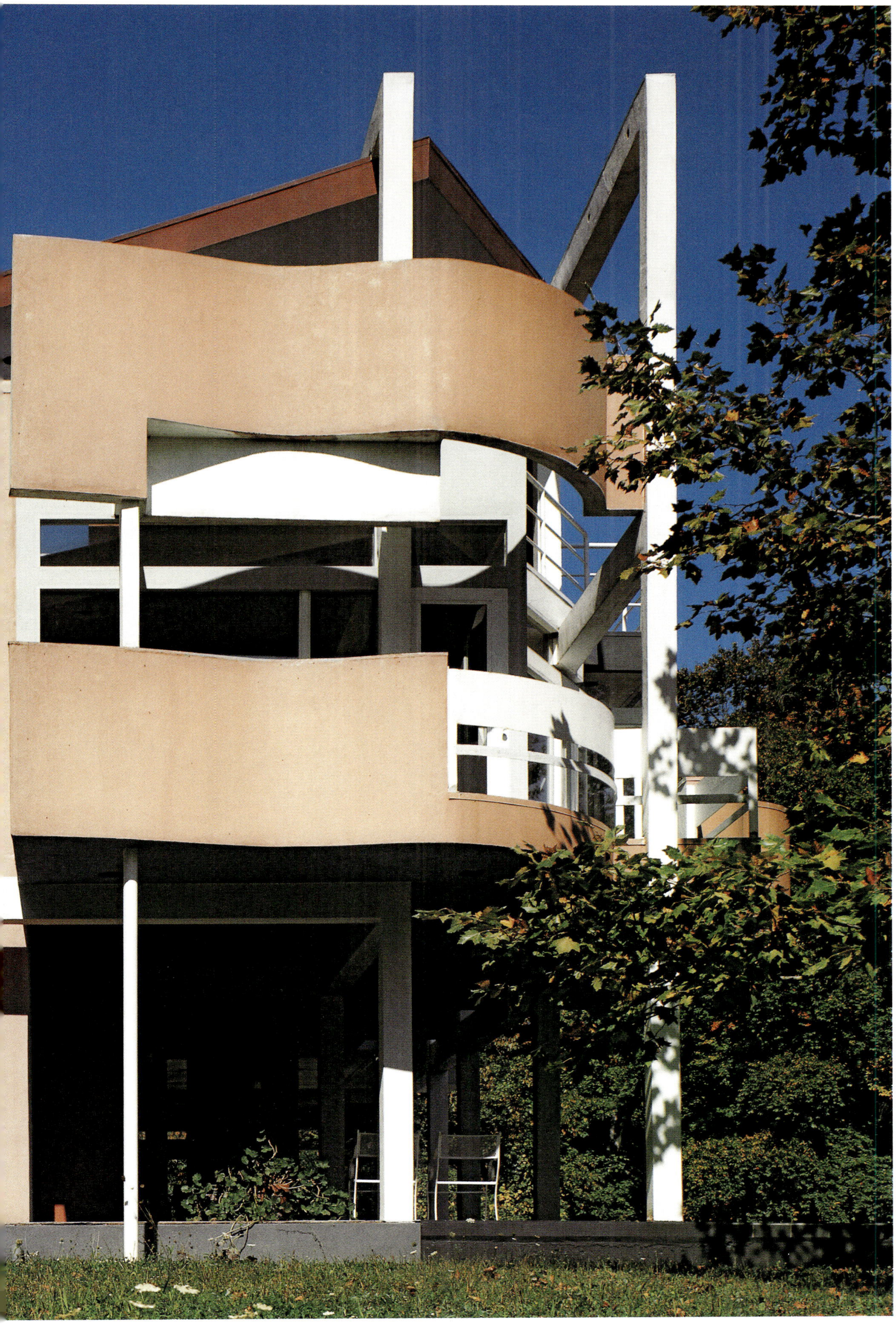

East elevation

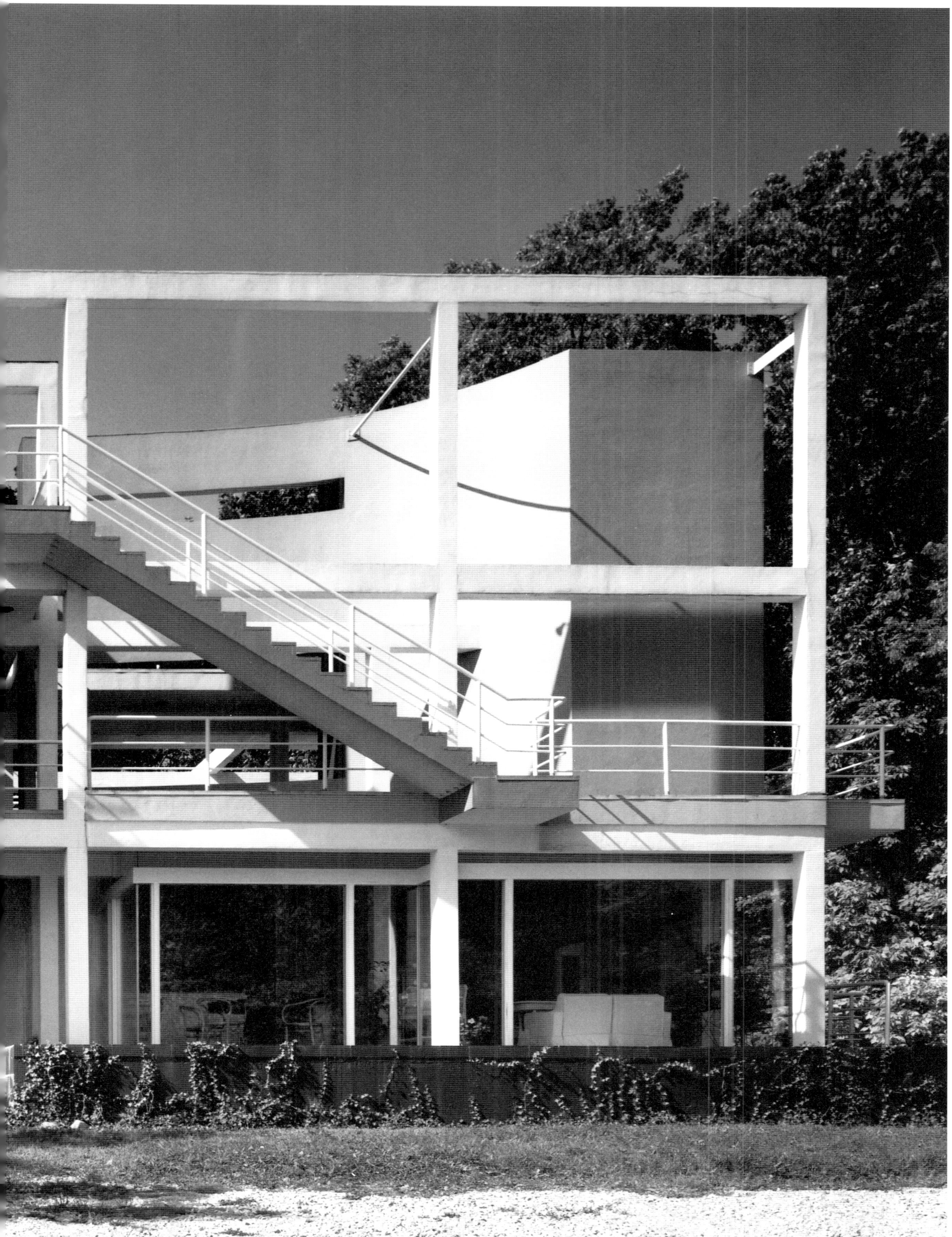

Terrace on east. Looking north

Terrace on southeast corner. Looking west

Roof terrace

Entrance terrace. View toward breakfast room

Entrance terrace. Entrance on right

Living room

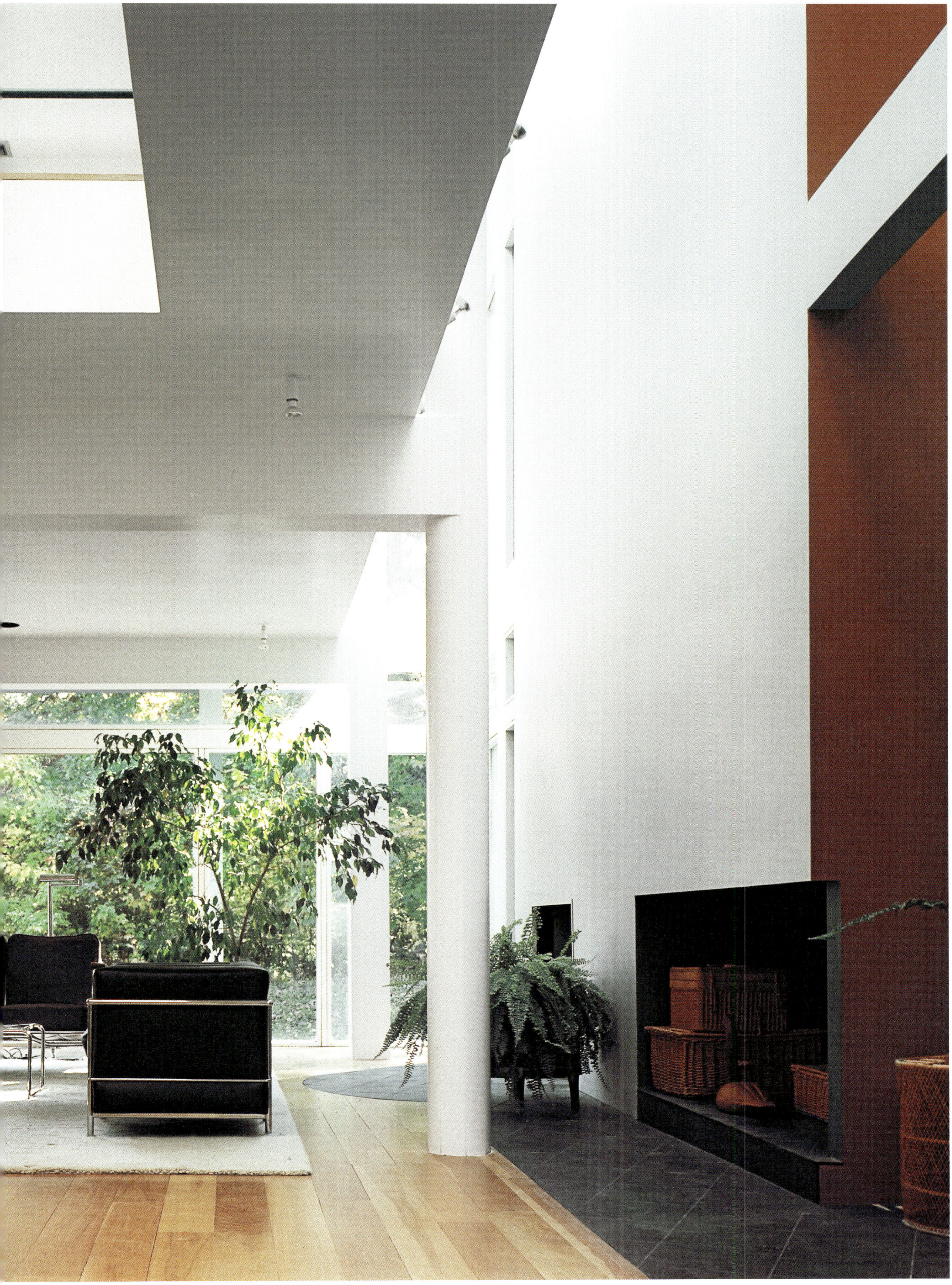

Living room. View toward entrance

Void at living room. Fireplace on right

Dining room. Living room on left

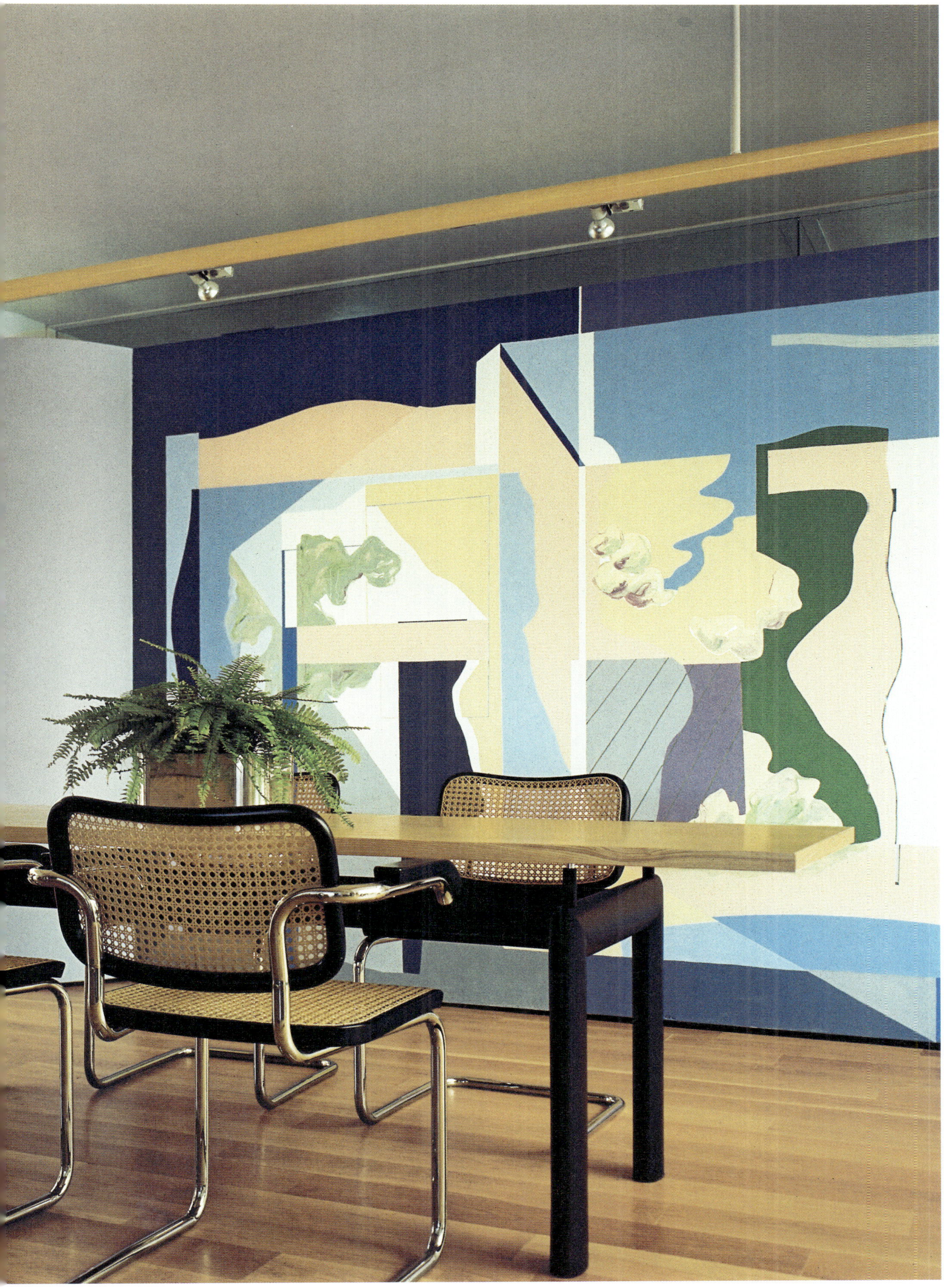

Dining room. Mural by Michael Graves

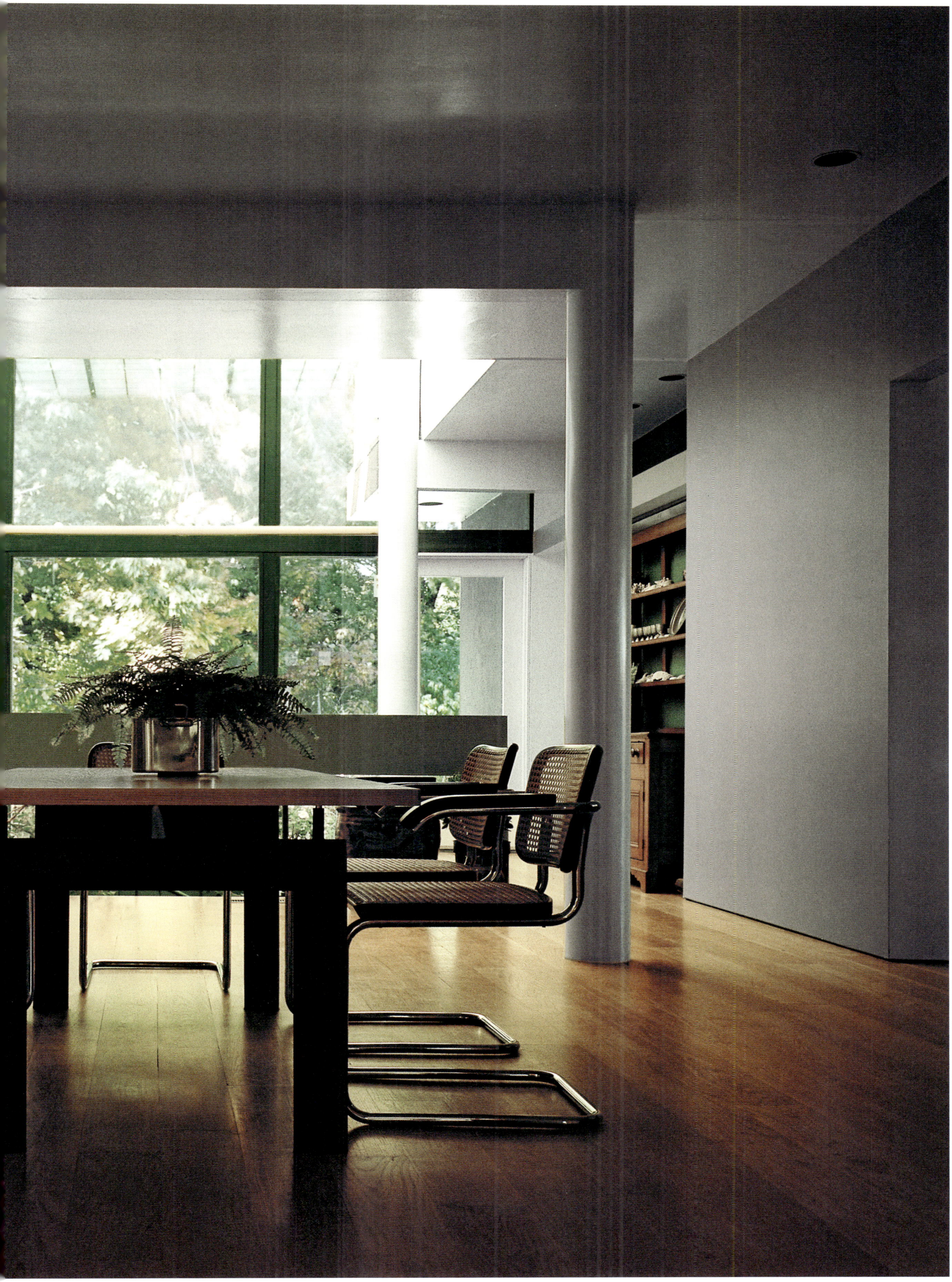

Staircase to second floor. Living room on left

Staircase to second floor

Second floor

Second floor. Staircase

pp.38-63: photos by T. Kitajima

世界現代住宅全集14
マイケル・グレイヴス
ハンセルマン邸
スナイダーマン邸

2013年5月24日発行
文：ジュリー・ハンセルマン・デイヴィーズ
企画・編集：二川幸夫
撮影：二川幸夫／GA photographers
アート・ディレクション：細谷巖
印刷・製本：大日本印刷株式会社
制作・発行：エーディーエー・エディタ・トーキョー
151-0051　東京都渋谷区千駄ヶ谷3-12-14
TEL.（03）3403-1581（代）

禁無断転載
ISBN 978-4-87140-639-0 C1352